INSTRUCTIONS: COUNSEL FOR NOVICES

St. Ammonias the Hermit

Translated by: D.P. Curtin

Dalcassian Publishing Company

PHILADELPHIA, PA

ISBN: 978-1-960069-66-5 (Paperback)

Library of Congress Control Number:
Author: Curtin, D.P. (1985-)

Front cover image: *Saint Sisoës the Great at the tomb of Alexander the Great (16th c., Varlaam Monastery, Meteora)*
Book design by J.J. Ripplestick

Printed by Ingram Content Group, 1 Ingram Blvd, La Vergne, Tennessee

First printing edition 2023.

1. — THE TEACHINGS OF OUR HOLY FATHER, AMMONIAS

There are four such things, that if man has any of them, he cannot repent, and God does not accept his prayer.

1. Pride first: when a man thinks that he lives well, that his conduct pleases God and men, that many are blessed when they encounter him, so much so that he has certainly delivered from many from fishing by withdrawing into the desert; if a man thinks these things, God does not dwell with him. It is rather that the monk condemns himself more than beings without reason, and that his works do not please God. It is said, in fact, by the 4th prophet: "All the justice of man is, in his presence, like the rag of a woman who has her rules". If the soul does not bear witness in truth, then it is more sinful than beings without reason like the birds and dogs. God will not accept his prayer. For beings without reason, dogs and birds have never sinned before God and will not be judged. It is obvious from this that the sinful man is more unhappy than the animals. It would be useful to him not to rise from among the dead, like beings of no reason, and not to come to judgment. Animals do not babble. They are not proud, and they love those who feed them. Yet, man does not love as he should, the God who made him and who feeds him.

2. Second, if anyone has a grudge against any man, even if he had lifted his eyes, preserved from resentment, hir prayer does not go up to God. Let him not flatter himself, even if he rises from the dead, apart from pity or forgiveness near God.

3. Thirdly, if anyone condemns a sinner, he himself will be condemned, even though he should do signs and wonders. For Christ said: "Judge not and you shall not be judged". The Christian must therefore judge no one, for the Father himself judges no one, but he left all judgment to the Son, so that he who judges before Christ is an Antichrist. Many of those who are thieves and fornicators today will be holy and righteous tomorrow, for we see their sins, but we do not know their hidden virtues and we judge them unjustly.

4. Fourth, if you have no charity. without it indeed, as the Apostle says, "even if we speak the languages of the angels, and we hold all true faith, even though we move mountains and give all we have to the poor, even if we would deliver our body to martyrdom, all that will be of no use to us." But you may say, "How can you give all you have to the poor and not have charity, for almsgiving is none other than charity?" Yet, almsgiving is not perfect charity; it is only a part of charity. Many give in charity to some and wrong to others, they harbor and hold grudges against others, protect some and insult others, sympathize with strangers and hate their relatives. In truth, this is not charity. For charity hates no one, insults no one, condemns no one, saddens no one, hates no one; neither the faithful, nor the unfaithful, nor the stranger, nor the sinner, nor the immodest, nor the proud, but she rather loves sinners, the weak and the careless. It is for them that she suffers, that she mourns and weeps. She sympathizes with the wicked and the sinners rather than with the good in imitation of Christ who called sinners by eating and drinking with them. Therefore, when he showed what true charity was, he taught it, saying: "Become good and merciful, like your Father, your heavenly father. Just as he sends rain on the bad and on the good and causes his sun to rise on the just and on the unjust, so he who has charity in all truth loves everyone, pities everyone, prays for everyone. There are indeed those who, it is true, give alms, but those who are convinced in that alone, commit many sins, hate many people and defile their bodies. They are deceiving themselves, by gaining consolation for themselves in the alms they would like to do.

2. — EXHORTATIONS

1. Take heed, my dear friend, because you have the confidence and the conviction that Our Lord Jesus Christ, who is God, and who has an ineffable glory and greatness, has made himself our model for us to walk in his footsteps. He humbled himself profoundly and beyond all expression for us by taking the form of the slave, without recoiling before profound poverty or before reproaches. He also endured many insults and grievances, and, as it is written: "He was led like a sheep to the slaughter and, as the lamb is speechless before the one shearing it, still he did not open the mouth." It is in humiliation that his judgment was consummated. He endured death with many outrages for us. So that we also, according to his command, must bear with good grace, for our own sins, if anyone, rightly or wrongly, outrages us, despises us, wrongs us, insults us and beats us to death. So, like a lamb led to the slaughter, and like an animal without a silence with great humility.

2. Take heed, believing that the insults, the slights and the humiliations which happen for the Lord's sake, are a great profit and the salvation of your soul; bear them with a good heart and without trouble, saying to yourself: "I deserve to suffer even more because of my sins; it is even a great deal for me to have you judged worthy to suffer and to endure For the Lord's sake; perhaps through many afflictions and humiliations I will imitate, at least in some way, the passion of my God. Whenever you remember those who have relied on you, pray for them all from the bottom of your soul and in truth, as having brought you great gain, and think nothing against anyone. But if someone honors you and praises you, grieves and prays to be rid of this burden, like anything that involves even a little glory and power. Pray unceasingly to God from the bottom of your soul and in all truth, that he removes all similar things from you, thinking that you are unworthy and crippled. Always seek diligently the

humblest ways of being and doing your work. Live in that with compassion and humility and without regret, as if you were going to die, and if you were already dead to this world; Live as if you were the last of all and the greatest sinner. All this, indeed, will be a great profit for your soul.

3. Beware what you hate and abhor, as if it were a terrible death to the loss of your soul, and eternal punishment. All desire for power and glory, and the desire for honors, distinctions and praises among men, and to think that you are something, that you are virtuous, or that you are more beautiful than average man, or the equal of so-and-so, and to think of everything shameful-desire and any carnal pleasure. However little, to observe a man without need, and to touch another body without need, and to tell someone "Where is that" without need, or to eat very little when you are not in need. You will do this, so long as you are guarded and strengthened in the smallest of things. You do not fall into sin more seriously but be sure that you are not tempted and that you do not fall little by little by despising the little things.

4. Be careful to truly ask for forgiveness of your sins, and to seek the salvation of your soul and the kingdom of heaven. Strive with all your might, in thought, word and the works, by dress and deportment, to observe humility, and to lower yourself like the soil, the earth and ashes. As the least among us is the servant of all, to look at you always, from the depth of the heart and in truth, like the last and most sinful of Christians, far removed from all virtue. Say to yourself: "In comparison with a Christian, I am only earth and ashes and like the rag of a menstruating woman, and it is only by great favor and grace that I can find mercy before God, as I am more worthy of punishment for eternal life. For those who want to enter into judgment, do not then have the way, seeing that I am full of abjection." While you hold your soul thus in mourning and humiliation and await death each day, pray unceasingly to God, that with great

mercy he may correct your soul and take pity on you, that you may you feel overwhelmed under the mourning and moaning, so that you never rejoice and laugh, but your laughter is always changed into pain and your joy into sadness; always walks with a gloomy air saying to you: my soul has been covered with mockery'.

5. Take care not to regard yourself, think of yourself as the last and most sinful of Christians, and to always hold your soul in pain, humiliation and groaning. Be silent always and do not speak. Have in mind the eternal darkness and those who are punished and tormented therein, judging yourself rather worthy of being one of these than of life, as if you deserved such punishment. From here below, as long as it is the moment of penance, to avoid these dreadful and great punishments, as if you were already dead and found yourself in this place in your mind. Hasten to grasp this continual pain with the weeping and all the great sorrow and sadness. Get yourself, in the order of the will of God, tired and fatigue in the soul and body. Accomplish them without becoming weary because of your illness, and keep your body without interruption, as much as you can, in manual labor, fasting and other numerous acts of humility according to God. Fulfill the word: "He who is master of all, must be servant to all" and hold in your soul always an unceasing meditation on the Scriptures. After a short interval of meditation, groan and pray long, be in the same frame of mind as if you were constantly attending the divine liturgy, so that the demons do not find the occasion to throw bad thoughts into your heart.

6. Take heed, in the conviction that our Lord died for us, rose again, and redeemed us with his blood, that we may not live for us. For the Lord who died and rose again for us, and again in the confidence and the persuasion that you are always before his eyes. Die to yourself and go out into this world as if you remained before him and remained there always.

7. Take heed, so that, as a servant accompanies his master with fear and trembling, and with great humility without moving away from him. Always be ready to listen to his will as well, whether you are sitting or standing, whether you are alone or with someone, you arrange to be always as before God, with fear and great trembling, for the body and for the soul, in order to always keep your body and your soul in fear and dread. As far as you can, let your mind be purified from unclean thoughts and from all reproach. Stand, in the presence of him who looks at you, with deep humility, gentleness, respect, tact, and with great knowledge of your station, without daring to look up because of your own iniquity.

8. Take good care, as if you dwelt and were always in the presence (of God) and be ready to obey his will, whether for life or for death, or for any affection, with much good will and faith, as if you were always expecting great and dreadful temptations to come to you, and even greater, dreadful afflictions, tortures and a frightful death.

9. Take heed, that in all that befalls you, whether in word, or deed, or thought, you in no way seek your will or your own respite, but carefully seek the will of God and that you desire to accomplish it entirely, even if it seems to you to entail affliction and death. For his commandment is eternal life.

10. Take good care, as if you were always in the presence of God, not to do anything without taking his advice. Whatever you want to do, either eat, or drink, or sleep, or visit someone, take heed to inquire first whether it be according to God's will. You will then act as one should do in the presence of God, so that by confessing Him thus in all your speeches and in all your actions

you will have, by this means, a great affection towards Him and a great assiduity.

11. Take heed, knowing that it is written: "We are useless servants, we do what it is our duty to do", so that in everything you do in works according to God, you do not do it for a salary. but in all humility, as if you were in truth a useless servant, and as if you were a debtor of a large sum of money. Whatever you do, look at yourself as lowly and as if you were adding to your sins almost every day because of your negligence. For he who knows how to do what is right, and who does not do it, commits a sin. For all that you omit from the commandments of God, you must always groan and pray to God assiduously and without interruption, so that with great mercy and philanthropy, he will forgive you your sins and have mercy on you.

12. Take good care to be silent when something afflicts you, and if it is a matter of pain, or some reason to be angry happens to you, say nothing beyond what is proper, until your heart is once again calmed. First be sweetened by continual prayer, only then will you pray to your brother. If you need to reprimand a brother, and if you see that he is angry and upset, don't say anything to him, lest he be even more upset in his anger. Yet, if you see that you and him are in great peace and forbearance, then talk to him at last, not by reprimanding him, but by warning him in all humility and gentleness, so as not to say a word in the anger of your mouth. Struggle always by being persuaded and believing that you are before the eyes of God and are seen by him everywhere. Dread him and fear him, knowing that in comparison with his unspeakable glory and his greatness, you will be as if you were nothing, earth and ashes, putrefaction and worms.

13. Take heed, believing that the Lord, for our sake, when he was generous, died for us, rose again, and redeemed us with his blood, in all redemption. You no longer live for yourself, but for the Lord. Be his perfect servant in everything, in order finally to attain complete calm. Like a very gentle animal who submits without resistance to his master, always stands before God, completely dead to human passions and to all pleasure, without ever having any desire or will of your own. Let all your will and all your desire always do the will of God, so as never to regard yourself as free or as your own master, but to say to yourself: "I am the servant of God, and he must submit to his will and do it." Behave as if you waited every day for a trial to come to you. Danger of death, or friendships, or great perils will come to pass, but endure them with good will and without trouble, thinking that through many tribulations we must enter the kingdom of heaven.

14. Take good care, as being always in the presence of God, so that in all that will happen to you, either in word, or in deed, or in thought, you do not seek your will nor your rest, but that you seek entirely, with care, the will of God. Though it may seem to involve labor, as if it were in truth the kingdom of heaven and the crown of life. Seek it out perfectly and carry it out always, believing wholeheartedly that his will trumps all human wisdom. For the precept of the Lord is eternal life, and those who love him shall not be deprived of any good.

15. Take good care, in order, as you were always in the presence of God, to do nothing without taking his advice. Whatever you want to do, either work, or talk, however small, visit someone or confer with him, sleep or do anything else, be cautious to find out first if it is necessary. Determine if it is you or whether it is God's will. So you shall give thanks before God with fear and with great trembling, that you may thus have a true union and relationship with God.

Give thanks in all your words and all your actions; and if you are aware that you have done something against these commandments, strive to repent, to grieve, and to pray to God to correct you, so that in judging yourself you will not soon fall.

16. Take good care, as if you were always in the presence of God, not to hope for anything from anyone except from the Lord alone with faith. In everything you need, pray to God that what you lack will happen to you, according to his will. And, in everything that happens to you, always praise God, as if it were He alone who gave it to you. If you lack something, without putting your hope in man at all, do not complain at all and do not murmur against anyone, but bear them courageously and without trouble, saying to yourself: "I deserve this trial and because of my own iniquity, but if God wants to take pity on me, he can; and in a short time, and in a short time, fill all my indigence.

17. Be careful not to receive or accept anything that does not test and prove what God gives you. What you see coming from the fruit of righteousness and with great peace and charity, accept it. Yet, whatever you see comes from injustice and with strife, fraud and hypocrisy, reject it saying to yourself: "Better is a small portion with the fear of the Lord, than much fruit with injustice."

18. Take good care, as if your great exercise and your great study were always to be silent and to practice not speaking at all. However little, do not say to someone: "Where is that?" If you need to say something, first examine in yourself whether there is a reasonable necessity, and if it is the will of God and then speak, because it is better for you in this case than to not talk. So confess to God the cause of the speech you wish to make, and so then, as if to obey the will of God, open your mouth to the word of God and speak, either to the

small or to the large, with all humility and meekness. While you speak, occupy your face and your mind with chaste and modest speech so that, if you meet someone, you will say a word or two to him with charity and then you will remain silent. And if you are asked something out of necessity, obey and nothing more.

19. Take good care to keep away from the concupiscence of the eyes, the hearing of the ears, and the mouth, as you keep away from fornication. So that you keep your eyes fixed on your work only, without looking up, except when you have a good reason. Do not direct your attention to a woman or a man with a beautiful face, unless it is absolutely necessary. Do not let your ears hear anything against anyone, or take in useless speeches. Let your mouth always be silent, that in doing so you may find mercy before the Lord God, who's glory and power endure forever and ever. Amen.

3. — DISCOURSE BY FATHER AMMONIAS ON THOSE WHO WANT TO LIVE IN SOLITUDE

1. To love to read the Scripture frivolously breeds discord and strife. Weeping over one's sins brings peace. It is, indeed, a sin for the monk who remains in his cell to read Scripture frivolously, neglecting his own sins. Whoever applies his heart to knowing what Scripture bears, this or that, before possessing himself first, he occupies his soul with superfluous care and falls into a multitude of exceedingly great captivity. While he who watches out not to be captive loves to prostrate himself before God. Whoever seeks out a likeness of God blasphemes God; but whoever seeks honor, loves purity in the fear of God. Whoever keeps the words of God knows God and observes them as a duty. Do not search the depths of God, as long as you pray to God to come to your aid, so that he enters into you and saves you from sin. For the gifts of God come outright, if the place is clear and forbidden to the profane.

2. He who clings to his own senses, clings to his own will, and acquires enmity and cannot escape the thoughts that bring sadness to the heart. Whoever sees the words of Scripture and observes them according to his own science, leans on it to say: "It is thus". This he ignores his own glory and this true wealth. Yet, he who sees and says: "I do not know, for I am a man", gives glory to God. The wealth of God dwells in him according to his strength.

3. "Do not agree to develop your reasoning in front of everyone, but only in front of your Fathers, so as not to draw sadness into your heart. Keep your mouth closed, so that your neighbor may be respected by you. Exercise your tongue on the words of God with prudence, and falsehood will flee from you.

4. Loving human glory breeds lies, while destroying it with humility increases the fear of God in the heart.

5. Desire not to become a friend of the nobles of the world, lest the glory of God be dulled in you.

6. If someone speaks badly of his brother in front of you, remove yourself from him and avoid his bad luck, you will not agree to go with him, for fear that what you do not want will happen to you . Simplicity and not measuring oneself purifies the heart from bad things. The pain of the heart will not spare him who deceives his brother.

7. If someone says one thing and has another wrong in his heart, the whole liturgical office of that one is in vain. Do not associate yourself with such a man, lest he defile you with his impure venom.

8. Walk with the good, so that you share in their glory and their purity.

9. Compassion with science begets foresight and leads to charity. Harshness shows that this one does not have virtue in him.

10. Kindness begets purity, but quarrels engender passions. Hardness of the heart breeds anger.

11. The exercise of the soul is to hate distraction. Exercise of the body is scarce.

12. Decline of the mind comes from the love of distractions. Loneliness in knowledge is the straightening of the spirit.

13. The satiety of sleep causes the tumult of the passions in the body. Insomnia with measure is the salvation of the heart. Lots of sleep weighs you down the e heart; but a propitious insomnia relieves him. Much sleep darkens the mind;

but insomnia with measure enlightens him. He who sleeps in silence, in knowledge, prevails over he who watches in vain talk.

14. Pain drives away all wickedness without trouble. Not hurting the feeling of the neighbor engenders humility.

15. The glory of men engenders pride little by little, and loving ostentation drives out knowledge.

16. The temperance of the belly destroys the passions, but the desire for food develops them without difficulty.

17. The adornment of the body is the death of the spirit, but it is good to deal with it according to the fear of God.

18. Heeding the judgments of God engenders fear of God in the soul but trampling on the conscience tears away the virtues of the heart.

19. Charity according to God banishes security, but security awakens it.

30. Watching your mouth elevates the mind to God, if it keeps silence intelligently, but talkativeness breeds negligence and madness.

31. Sacrificing your will to your neighbor shows that your intelligence sees virtue, but maintaining your will against your neighbor denotes ignorance.

32. Meditation in fear guards the soul against the passions, but speaking the language of the world hides the virtues from him.

33. Loving the world troubles the mind and the soul. While the renunciation of the world renews intelligence and the soul.

24. Your silence when there is reason will reveal your thoughts, and shows that you seek the honor of the world and its evil glory. Yet. he who is not afraid to reveal his thoughts before his Fathers, casts them far from him.

25. Like a house that has no door or window, and where any reptile can enter as it pleases, so is he who does his work without paying his attention to it.

26. Like the rust that corrodes iron, so is the consideration of men, if the heart puts its trust in it.

27. Humility is at the head of all virtues, and gluttony is at the head of all passions.

28. Charity is the end of virtues, and to consider oneself just is the fullness of the passions.

29. As the worm that eats wood destroys it, so wickedness in the heart darkens the Soul from virtues.

30. Humbling the soul in the presence of God makes it possible to endure mistreatment without trouble, and the tears of the soul are saved from all human sorrows.

31. The absence of self-blaming leads to the absence of support.

32. Engaging in conversation with those in the world troubles the heart and confuses the one who prays to God, through lack of trust.

33. To love the profit of the world darkens the soul, while to despise it in everything leads to knowledge.

34. Love of work entails hatred of the passions, while laziness brings them without pain.

35. Do not cling to business, and your reason will be quiet within you.

36. Do not put your trust in your strength, otherwise the support of God will leave you.

37. Have no enmity against anyone, otherwise your prayer will not be accepted. Be at peace with all, so that you can abide in trust when you pray.

38. Keep your eyes, and your heart will see no evil. He who looks at anything with pleasure, commits adultery.

39. Do not desire to learn of the wrong that is done to you by him who insults you, lest you take it to heart.

40. Guard your ears, lest you get excited over conflict.

41. Commit to your manual work, so that the poor find your bread, for idleness is the death and fall of the soul.

42. Constant prayer destroys focus, but progressive neglect gives birth to oblivion.

43. He who has death in expectation will not sin as much, but he who promises himself a long life will be involved in many sins.

44. For the one who prepares to render an account to God of all his actions, God takes care to purify him from every marker of sin. The one who doesn't care and says he can go so far is adjacent to the wicked.

45. Every day, before doing any work, remember who you are and where you will go when you come out of the body; and you will not pass a day without taking care of your soul.

46. Think of the honor that all the saints have received, and their zeal will lead you little by little. Think again of the reproaches that the wicked have incurred, and you will keep yourself from bad things.

47. Always take the advice of the Fathers, and you will spend all the time in control of your life.

48. Take heed if your thoughts torment you because a brother is afflicted against you, do not despise him, but repent to him with a pleading voice, until you are able to persuade him. Make sure he is not hardened against you, for we are all overcome by enmity.

49. If you live with brothers, do not command them in everything, but work with them, so as not to lose your calm.

50. If the demons disturb you on the occasion of food and clothing and subject you to the reproach of great poverty, do not answer them in anything, but take refuge in God with all your heart, and you find rest.

51. See that you do not forget to perform your liturgical services, for they lead to the illumination of the spirit.

52. If you have done good deeds, do not brag about it. If you have done many evils, let your heart not be saddened beyond measure, but watch over your heart so that you are no longer captivated by this evil, and you will be guarded against pride in your wisdom.

53. If you are tormented by impurity, burden your body constantly in humility before God and do not let your heart believe that your sins have been forgiven you, and you find rest.

54. If gluttony leads you to desire certain foods, remember their bad smell, and you find rest.

55. If backbiting pushes you against your brother, remember that if you listen to him there will be cause for complaint, if you give up walking against him you will find rest.

56. If pride dominates you, remember that if you lose all your work, and there is no penance for those who listen to you, and you find rest.

57. If contempt arises in your will against your neighbor, remember that God will therefore deliver you into the hands of your enemies, and you find rest.

58. If the beauty of the body arouses your body, remember its stench when it dies, and you find rest.

59. If you are oppressed by the pleasure of women, as if it were very pleasant to you, remember where those who are already dead have been and you will find rest.

60. In all these things indeed discernment,1 making deductions and reasoning, makes good things prosper and bad things ineffective. It is impossible for

discernment to come if you do not do all that accompanies it, including liturgy. First seek solitude. There, loneliness engenders asceticism and tears, tears breed fear, fear begets humility and foresight. Foresight engenders charity, and charity makes the soul healthy and impassive. Then man understands that after all these things, he is not far from God.

61. Therefore those who want to have access to these dignities of virtue will remain without concern, far from any man, so as not to judge him, and he will prepare himself for death. Each time he prays, he seeks what separates him from God and it will render him ineffectual. He will hate this world, and the goodness of God will soon give him the virtues. He will learn that any man who drinks and eats without discretion, or who loves something of this world, will not have access to the virtues, and in not obtaining them, he deceives himself.

62. I therefore beg everyone who wants to do penance for God to beware of drunkenness, because it renews all the passions and drives the fear of God far from the soul.

63. However, with all your strength, ask God to send you his fear, so that by your desire is directed towards God alone, you will extirpate all the passions which fight against the unfortunate soul, seeking to separate it from God in order to fully possess it. This is no doubt why the enemies fight with all their might by attacking man.

64. So do not seek rest, brother, while you are in the body in this world, and do not take confidence in yourself in the short time of passions, because the enemies' tricks are contained for a time. Deceivers as they are, until man has loosened his heart and his thinking is at rest. Then they spring suddenly on an unfortunate soul, seize it like a sparrow and, if they prevail over it, they humiliate it pitilessly in all its sins. It is much more difficult to obtain forgiveness of these things, than of those for which were prayed for in the beginning.

65. Let us therefore keep ourselves in fear of God and take care to exercise our activity by observing all the virtues which prevent the malice of the enemies, because the labors and the sufferings of this short life not only keep us from evil, but still prepare the crowns of the soul before it leaves the body.

66. Let us therefore flee, my brothers, from the world and what is in it, so that we inherit treasure in heaven. For the heritage of this world is gold and silver, houses and clothes. Not only do all these things cause us to sin, but we give them up when we leave this world. The heritage of God is immense. Eye did not see it, ear did not hear it, it did not come into the mind of man, and God gave it to those who listen to it in this short life among those who do not seek it in idleness, but with the help of the bread, the water and the clothes which they gave to those who were in need, with the help of philanthropy, purity, and of the body far from corruption. It is right if one does not harm one's neighbor, if one keeps one's mind pure, if one observes all his other precepts.

67. Those who observe these things will find rest. Men will honor them in this world and will receive eternal glory when they leave their body.

68. As for those who do their will in sin and do not want to repent, who are distracted from pleasures, who accomplish their wickedness by deceiving themselves, with the buffoonery of their speech, their vociferations in their quarrels, contempt for the judgment of God, harshness towards the poor and all other sins, their faces of will be covered with confusion in this world, and men will despise them. When they go out of this world, they will be reproached with shame, and will be driven into Gehenna.

69. Yet, God can strengthen us and give us the grace to advance in his works by preserving us from all evil works, so that we can be saved in the hour of the trial which must fall on everyone.

70. For Our Lord Jesus Christ will not delay, but he will come bringing payment. He will send the wicked to eternal fire, and he will give the reward to his own and they will enter with him and they will rest in his kingdom every hour. Amen.

71. So don't lose heart, brother, read this every day. Perhaps we will also find mercy with those whom Christ judges worthy.

72. Take care therefore, my dear friend, to observe these serious commandments, so that you may be saved with the saints who have observed the precepts of Our Lord Jesus Christ. Yet, if someone reads them and does not

observe them, he is like someone who sees his face in a mirror and immediately forgets what he was.

73. But if anyone reads these things and acts upon them, he is like the good seed which is sown in the good ground and which bears fruit. God can cause us to be found by those who listen and who observe, so that he also receives from us the fruit of our labors, and is saved by his grace, for to him is the strength, the glory and the power in age of all ages. Amen.

Other Titles by D.P. Curtin:

First Book of Ethiopian Maccabees (2018)
Instructions: Counsel for Novices by St. Ammonas the Hermit (2022)
The Syriac Menologium and Martyrology (2022)
Book on Religious Exercise and Quiet by St. Isaiah the Solitary (2022)
Vision of Theophilus by St. Cyril of Alexandria (2022)
On Fate (De Fato) by St. Albertus Magnus (2023)
Fragments of 'Chronicle' by Hippolytus of Thebes (2023)
Life of the Blessed Theotokos by Epiphanius Monachus (2023)
Syriac Life of John the Baptist by Serapion the Presbyter (2023)
Second Book of Ethiopian Maccabees (2023)